31 Prayers for Healing

Nathaniel Turner

DEDICATION

To my dear friend David, who suffered the loss of his father to illness in February 2004.

CONTENTS

ACKNOWLEDGMENTS

My gratitude goes to God, above all, Who caused me to grow through illness and Who led me to peace in spite of that disease. I also want to thank my wife for her support and my parents for their help in troubled times.

AUTHOR'S NOTE

What I have written here is meant to help the reader vocalize his or her prayers to the Lord directed by the Word of God. I have introduced each prayer with the phrase, "Dear Lord," and finished them with the phrase, "In Thy Son's Name I pray, AMEN," which is my own custom. Both the prayers themselves and the introductory and concluding words are meant to be a guide only; feel free to supplement or alter these prayers for your personal use.

Prayers for healing are a tricky matter. Do not presume that, if you pray one or more of these prayers, that you will immediately be healed of every ailment. Sometimes, illness is part of God's plan for our lives, which means that we must endure it instead of whisking it away with a quick prayer. These prayers are as much for peace and acceptance of illness as they are for healing. Keep this in mind.

It is my intention that these prayers assist the reader in his or her personal prayer life and help him or her to speak to God when he or she cannot find the words. If the reader does wish to pray publicly what I have written here, I would appreciate a mention that it was I who wrote it.

Please feel free to visit the 31 Prayers website at
http://www.31Prayers.com
to find out about past and future installments in the 31 Prayers series and to post your comments and questions about this book.

HEALING THROUGH OBEDIENCE AND RIGHTEOUSNESS

Deuteronomy 7:12, 15

"Then it shall come about, because you listen to these judgments and keep and do them, that the LORD your God will keep with you His covenant and His lovingkindness which He swore to your forefathers... The LORD will remove from you all sickness; and He will not put on you any of the harmful diseases of Egypt which you have known, but He will lay them on all who hate you."

2

Dear Lord,

Help me to listen to Your judgments and do them; help me to follow Your commandments, fulfilling the part of Israel in Your covenant, that I may participate in that covenant and receive the blessings of Your lovingkindness. Remove from me all sickness and cleanse me from disease; protect me from the plagues You have placed on Egypt and on all those who hate Your chosen people. Shield me and purify me, O LORD; cleanse me from my sin and heal my illness that You may be glorified.

In Thy Son's Name I pray, AMEN.

Matthew 8:16-17

When evening came, they brought to Him many who were demon-possessed; and He cast out the spirits with a word, and healed all who were ill. This was to fulfill what was spoken through Isaiah the prophet: "He Himself took our infirmities and carried away our diseases."

Dear Lord,

I am ill and weak with infirmities. I bring myself before You, as many were brought before You in Capernaum. You took upon Yourself our griefs and our sorrows, our infirmities and our diseases. O LORD, I ask You to take away my illness and to heal me. Take away, too, my sin and wash me of my iniquity. Help me to become pure in body and soul as Christ is pure. Help me to see the impurities of the flesh as only that; let me not be fooled into assuming Your ire or hatred, as Isaiah warned and as the friends of Job were fooled. Lead me instead to put my trust and hope in You, Who cleanse me from sin and pain.

In Thy Son's Name I pray, AMEN.

John 9:6-7

When He had said this, He spat on the ground, and made clay of the spittle, and applied the clay to his eyes, and said to him, "Go, wash in the pool of Siloam" (which is translated, Sent). So he went away and washed, and came back seeing.

Dear Lord,

Obedience to Your will is difficult for me. I am not easily able to humble myself and risk what I have made so that You may give me what You desire for me. Help me to realize that I am as a beggar in the street before You; help me to know that what I have done is only what You have given me the power to do. Help me to learn obedience and to submit to Your holy and righteous will, O God, that I may be healed by Your power and made whole once more.

In Thy Son's Name I pray, AMEN.

HEALING THROUGH FAITH AND REPENTANCE

II Chronicles 7:13-14

If I shut up the heavens so that there is no rain, or if I command the locust to devour the land, or if I send pestilence among My people, and My people who are called by My name humble themselves and pray and seek My face and turn from their wicked ways, then I will hear from heaven, will forgive their sin and will heal their land.

Dear Lord,

I am fallen. I have sinned in Your sight; against You only have I sinned. I seek Your forgiveness; I seek to turn away from my sin and to be purified. As Israel sinned against You and brought Your righteous wrath upon themselves, so my sins condemn my soul and plague my flesh. I know that I am sinful, and I pray now; I seek Your face, O LORD, and I strive to turn from my wicked ways. Hear my plea from heaven, O God, and heal my land, which You alone have given unto me.

In Thy Son's Name I pray, AMEN.

Psalm 39:7, 10-11

"And now, Lord, for what do I wait?
My hope is in You....

"Remove Your plague from me;
Because of the opposition of Your hand I am perishing.

"With reproofs You chasten a man for iniquity;
You consume as a moth what is precious to him;
Surely every man is a mere breath."

Dear Lord,

I suffer and wait, O LORD. I hope only in You. In my sin, You have reproached me. In my failures, You have reminded me of the right path. Remove from me the plague which You have placed upon me for reproof. You are just and holy, tempered by love; I appeal to You for forgiveness and healing, O God, for I am perishing because of the opposition of Your hand. You have sent Your Son to die for my sins, through Whom You may gaze upon me as righteous. My hope is by Him fulfilled; save me from my sin and, for Your glory, heal me of my pain.

In Thy Son's Name I pray, AMEN.

Proverbs 3:5-8

Trust in the LORD with all your heart
And do not lean on your own understanding.
In all your ways acknowledge Him,
And He will make your paths straight.
Do not be wise in your own eyes;
Fear the LORD and turn away from evil.
It will be healing to your body
And refreshment to your bones.

Dear Lord,

Sin and folly are in my life. I suffer from both my own shortcomings and the afflictions of the flesh. Help me to turn away from my folly and to repent of my sins. I seek to trust You with my whole heart, and let me not lean on the broken limb of my own understanding. Help me to acknowledge You always and keep my eyes upon You as the prize, so that the light of Your presence will be a lamp unto my feet and will guide me on the straight path. Remind me that I am incomplete without You, that it is You whence my wisdom comes. Help me to fear You in righteousness and turn my back on the sin that plagues me. In all these things, O God, be healing unto my body and refreshment unto my bones; for Your Name's sake, cleanse me of illness and heal me of pain.

In Thy Son's Name I pray, AMEN.

Isaiah 57:18-19

"I have seen his ways, but I will heal him;
I will lead him and restore comfort to him and to his mourners,
Creating the praise of the lips.
Peace, peace to him who is far and to him who is near,"
Says the LORD, "and I will heal him."

Dear Lord,

I am the one contrite of heart, and I am the one of lowly spirit. I have often followed the way of my fallen heart, instead of what You have designed for me. LORD, do not always be angry with me; do not contend forever. Even though You know my ways, O God, heal me. Lead me and restore comfort to me and to those who mourn with me and over me, creating praise in our lips where once was grief. I may have wandered far from Your will, O LORD, but whether I am far from You or near, I ask Your healing. Purify me; cleanse me; cure me, O LORD. Heal me of my iniquities and my illness; make me well so that I will bring glory to Your name.

In Thy Son's Name I pray, AMEN.

Jeremiah 30:17

"For I will restore you to health
And I will heal you of your wounds," declares the LORD,
"Because they have called you an outcast, saying:
'It is Zion; no one cares for her.'"

Dear Lord,

Zion is Your holy city, O God, the city of Your servant David. It is the city of Your kingdom. But Jerusalem has fallen from Your grace, and Your people suffer in sin. In repentance I turn to You, O God; in sorrow I seek Your face. Others see my suffering and suppose that no one cares for me; they say that no one, least of all You, has any favor towards me. But LORD, at my lowest, at my weakest, in my moment of greatest suffering, restore to me my health and heal me of my wounds, not for my sake, but that I may glorify You, that in me sinners may be blessed by Your wondrous deeds of forgiveness and healing.

In Thy Son's Name I pray, AMEN.

HEALING THROUGH THE GRACE OF GOD

Psalm 147:3

*He heals the brokenhearted
And binds up their wounds.*

Dear Lord,

You are the kind and merciful one, O God, You Who heal the brokenhearted and bind up our sorrows. Many things in this life cause us pain. We suffer from illness and plague and disease. But You, O LORD, are great and worthy of praise; You, O LORD, are holy and just, loving and merciful. Have mercy on me, Father, for I am lost without You; take pity and heal me, for alone, I fall. My heart is broken by the suffering that my family and I must endure; I am wounded, and my sorrows harrow me. Heal me, O God, and bind up my wounds; save me for Your glory.

In Thy Son's Name I pray, AMEN.

Isaiah 53:5

But He was pierced through for our transgressions,
He was crushed for our iniquities;
The chastening for our well-being fell upon Him,
And by His scourging we are healed.

Dear Lord,

Your Son, Your Messiah, the Chosen and Anointed One, about Whom Your Spirit spoke through the prophets, has borne our suffering and our transgressions. You sent Him and made Him flesh, and He dwelt among us; He was tempted just as we are tempted, yet was without sin. He took our sins upon Himself and suffered under Your righteous hand for our sakes. By the scourging of His flesh, You take away the scourging of ours; although we were the ones who sinned, not Him, He was the One Who suffered above all, that we might not. Help me to remember what You have done for me, O LORD, and I pray that You strengthen me and heal me for Your Name's sake, that all may know that You are God.

In Thy Son's Name I pray, AMEN.

Matthew 9:20-22

And a woman who had been suffering from a hemorrhage for twelve years, came up behind Him and touched the fringe of His cloak; for she was saying to herself, "If I only touch His garment, I will get well." But Jesus turning and seeing her said, "Daughter, take courage; your faith has made you well." At once the woman was made well.

Dear Lord,

My illness has been paining me for a long time, and I often fear that I will never be rid of it. But I know that You are holy and righteous and powerful. I know, I trust, that if You still walked among us in the flesh, I would need only to touch Your garment—unworthy as I am to be touched by You—and I would be healed. I pray this healing faith in my life; I pray in earnest that I trust You fully, as the woman in the crowd trusted You. I pray the courage You offered her, that I may come into Your presence and ask Your mercy and Your healing power. Let me be, as this woman was, an example of faith inspired by Your holiness, that You may be glorified in me.

In Thy Son's Name I pray, AMEN.

Luke 18:38-42

And he called out, saying, "Jesus, Son of David, have mercy on me!" Those who led the way were sternly telling him to be quiet; but he kept crying out all the more, "Son of David, have mercy on me!" And Jesus stopped and commanded that he be brought to Him; and when he came near, He questioned him, "What do you want Me to do for you?" And he said, "Lord, I want to regain my sight!" And Jesus said to him, "Receive your sight; your faith has made you well."

Dear Lord,

I trust in You. I seek healing in Your will and by Your power. Let me cry out for Your mercy. Though others may tell me that You are too busy or too important for a wretch like me, though others may say that the time for miracles has gone and You will not heal me, let me evermore be persistent; let me cry out all the more in faith for Your mercy. And when You look upon me with grace, O LORD, grant me healing; by the faith You have instilled in me, O God, save me.

In Thy Son's Name I pray, AMEN.

John 5:5-9a

A man was there who had been ill for thirty-eight years. When Jesus saw him lying there, and knew that he had already been a long time in that condition, He said to him, "Do you wish to get well?" The sick man answered Him, "Sir, I have no man to put me into the pool when the water is stirred up, but while I am coming, another steps down before me." Jesus said to him, "Get up, pick up your pallet and walk." Immediately the man became well, and picked up his pallet and began to walk.

Dear Lord,

I find myself in illness for a long time; I find myself weak and at the mercy of others. O LORD, I have no means to acquire healing through the way of the world. My God, I sincerely do wish to become well, but I cannot see a way for me, when I am weak and without a savior. Intercede on my behalf, O God; have mercy upon me. Grant me healing against all odds, that I, like the man at the pool called Bethesda, may go and tell the world that it was You Who healed me. Thy will be done, O LORD.

In Thy Son's Name I pray, AMEN.

HEALING THROUGH THE POWER OF GOD

Psalm 73:26

My flesh and my heart may fail,
But God is the strength of my heart and my portion forever.

Dear Lord,

My fallen flesh is frail, O God. I cannot withstand the pains and sufferings of this world on my own. I am torn by wounds and I ache with illness. But You, O LORD, are greater than my sorrows; You, Who sent Your Son to suffer as we suffer, to be beset with weakness even as we ourselves are, You are most qualified of all to purify and cleanse me, body and soul, to be the strength of my heart through the indwelling of Your Spirit. O LORD, help me to be truly satisfied with Your presence; You are my portion and my cup, and if You would have me suffer for Your Name's sake, then You will be enough for me. Yet if You will heal me of my pains and cure my ills, then I would glorify You alone and bring honor to Your Name.

In Thy Son's Name I pray, AMEN.

Isaiah 45:22

"Turn to Me and be saved, all the ends of the earth;
For I am God, and there is no other."

Dear Lord,

Forgive me for thinking that I could accomplish what You alone may achieve. Let me not place myself or any other above You in power or worship, O LORD. But I ask You, Heavenly Father, to provide a doctor, medicine, or miracle to heal me of my illnesses and to wash away the plagues that have overwrought me. Let me turn from my sin, O God, let me seek Your face; save me from whatever circumstance has befallen me. For You are God, O LORD, and there is no other.

In Thy Son's Name I pray, AMEN.

Jeremiah 17:14

Heal me, O LORD, and I will be healed;
Save me and I will be saved,
For You are my praise.

Dear Lord,

You are powerful, O God; You are great. You spoke all of Creation into existence. Surely anything You say will be made so. You are my praise, O God; because of You alone am I at all worthy of the praise of others, and You above all others do I seek to praise. I am wounded and afflicted, O God of praise and power. Heal me, O LORD, and I will be healed; save me and I will be saved. As You will, so be it, my God.

In Thy Son's Name I pray, AMEN.

Matthew 9:2-6

And they brought to Him a paralytic lying on a bed. Seeing their faith, Jesus said to the paralytic, "Take courage, son; your sins are forgiven." And some of the scribes said to themselves, "This fellow blasphemes." And Jesus knowing their thoughts said, "Why are you thinking evil in your hearts? Which is easier, to say, 'Your sins are forgiven,' or to say, 'Get up, and walk'? But so that you may know that the Son of Man has authority on earth to forgive sins"—then He said to the paralytic, "Get up, pick up your bed and go home."

Dear Lord,

You are powerful, O God, and You are holy. Help me to recognize that true power and authority rests in You, Who have the capacity to forgive sins. Help me to recognize and accept this great and wonderful gift, so easy to say yet so difficult to enact. O LORD, in my illness, I pray, too, that You say to me, "Get up, and walk." Cure me of my ailments and heal me of my sickness. Because You have forgiven me, which is the first and better gift, I know You have the power and authority to heal my flesh also. If otherwise be Your will, I pray peace and acceptance in my heart and the hearts of my family, and I pray guidance in Your will that I might bring You glory.

In Thy Son's Name I pray, AMEN.

HEALING THROUGH GOD ALONE

Hosea 5:13, 15

When Ephraim saw his sickness,
And Judah his wound,
Then Ephraim went to Assyria
And sent to King Jareb.
But he is unable to heal you,
Or to cure you of your wound....

I will go away and return to My place
Until they acknowledge their guilt and seek My face;
In their affliction they will earnestly seek Me.

Dear Lord,

In my illness, O God, remind me, as the prophet Hosea reminded Your people Israel, that I cannot find healing apart from You. No other gods, be they of my own construction or of external origin, are able to cure me of my wound. O LORD, if I have sought refuge in wealth or science or philosophy or the machinations of mankind, forgive me. I am wounded as Ephraim and as Judah; I am sick. Heal me, O God, and cure me of my wound.

In Thy Son's Name I pray, AMEN.

HEALING FOR THE GLORY OF GOD

Ezekiel 34:15-16

"I will feed My flock and I will lead them to rest," declares the Lord GOD. "I will seek the lost, bring back the scattered, bind up the broken and strengthen the sick; but the fat and the strong I will destroy. I will feed them with judgment."

Dear Lord,

I pray that I am humble. In my grief and pain, I am lost, scattered by the winds of adversity; I am broken by my ills and sick with disease. O LORD, feed me and lead me to rest. Do not leave me in some delusion of strength on my own, but heal me of my pains, that I and all who see me may know that it is by Your hand that I live at all, that every gift is from You. Find me in my wayward paths, bring me back to the fold; bind up my bones and strengthen my limbs, that my illness fails and You and Your glory succeed.

In Thy Son's Name I pray, AMEN.

Mark 1:40-42

And a leper came to Jesus, beseeching Him and falling on his knees before Him, and saying, "If You are willing, You can make me clean." Moved with compassion, Jesus stretched out His hand and touched him, and said to him, "I am willing; be cleansed." Immediately the leprosy left him and he was cleansed.

Dear Lord,

I seek Your mercy in my time of need, O God. I come to You, LORD, beseeching You and falling on my knees before You. If You are willing, LORD, You can make me clean. I pray Your compassion, Father, and I pray this to be Your will. Touch my flesh with Your righteous hand and make me whole and clean once more. And help me to be, as this leper was, unable to contain the greatness of what You do for me; help me to proclaim it freely and to spread the news around, so that people come to You from everywhere. But not my will, but Yours be done, O God.

In Thy Son's Name I pray, AMEN.

Luke 17:12-19

*As He entered a village, ten leprous men who stood at a distance met Him;
and they raised their voices, saying, "Jesus, Master, have mercy on us!"
When He saw them, He said to them, "Go and show yourselves to the
priests." And as they were going, they were cleansed. Now one of them, when
he saw that he had been healed, turned back, glorifying God with a loud
voice, and he fell on his face at His feet, giving thanks to Him. And he was
a Samaritan. Then Jesus answered and said, "Were there not ten cleansed?
But the nine—where are they? Was no one found who returned to give glory
to God, except this foreigner?" And He said to him, "Stand up and go;
your faith has made you well."*

Dear Lord,

You are present in this world. I call out to You through Your Son, "Jesus, Master, have mercy on me!" Send me out into the world as living proof of Your power and mercy, as You sent the ten lepers, cleansing me as I go. But let me not be like the nine, O LORD, interested only in myself, as though I were responsible for my own wholeness. Let me instead be as the one, who returned to You in praise and thanks. Let me give glory not to myself, but to You, O God. Let me be exultant and overjoyed as I am filled with Your grace and Your mercy; let me cry out so that all may know that it is You, O LORD, who heal and make whole those whom man has rejected. Let me be as this one; grant me faith that I may be saved.

In Thy Son's Name I pray, AMEN.

I Corinthians 6:13

Food is for the stomach and the stomach is for food, but God will do away with both of them. Yet the body is not for immorality, but for the Lord, and the Lord is for the body.

Dear Lord,

I pray for healing, O LORD, that I may continue to work for Your will and glory. Even so, O God, remind me that Your plan extends beyond this life. Remind me that this body is for bodily things, but this body and this world will be made as nothing. I know that this flesh is weak and flawed, yet still I dedicate it to Your service, O LORD, for I know that You work in my favor, body, soul, and spirit, one person. Indeed, You do not hate bodies, for You did not eschew the flesh, but became flesh for us, that our flesh might be redeemed through the resurrection of the Christ. Whether You heal this mortal body or not, I dedicate it again to Your glory, that You may raise me up on the last day in a new, holy, immortal, and flawless body. God, grant me the peace to remain steadfast in this resolve.

In Thy Son's Name I pray, AMEN.

HEALING AND SALVATION

Psalm 34:19

Many are the afflictions of the righteous,
But the LORD delivers him out of them all.

Dear Lord,

I pray Your deliverance, O LORD. I seek to be counted among the righteous who follow You and are called by Your name. I suffer greatly, O God, and many are my afflictions. Deliver me, first, from my sins, through Jesus Christ Your Son, and second, from all my suffering and afflictions, that You may be glorified. Help me, O LORD, to remain faithful and righteous in Your eyes, and heal these pains for Your Name's sake.

In Thy Son's Name I pray, AMEN.

John 6:48-51

"I am the bread of life. Your fathers ate the manna in the wilderness, and they died. This is the bread which comes down out of heaven, so that one may eat of it and not die. I am the living bread that came down out of heaven; if anyone eats of this bread, he will live forever; and the bread also which I will give for the life of the world is My flesh."

Dear Lord,

You send us food to sustain our flesh, but I pray for the true Bread from Heaven, the Bread of life, to sustain my soul. My flesh is weak, O God, but Your Flesh is not. If it be Your will, I pray that You make my flesh whole, but whether I am healed in body or not, I seek earnestly the salvation of my soul. Grant me this Bread from Heaven, that I may eat it and not die, but have peace and joy and hope in You. Let me partake of You in Your Son, Jesus Christ, Who is the living Bread that grants eternal life. I pray for the healing of my body, Heavenly Father, but a healthy body is worthless without a healthy soul.

In Thy Son's Name I pray, AMEN.

HEALING AND UNITY

Luke 10:33-34

But a Samaritan, who was on a journey, came upon him; and when he saw him, he felt compassion, and came to him and bandaged up his wounds, pouring oil and wine on them; and he put him on his own beast, and brought him to an inn and took care of him.

Dear Lord,

I am wounded and gravely ill. Like a man beaten and robbed and left for dead, I am too weak to care for myself. O God, have mercy upon me. Send to me, not a chief priest, nor a Levite, nor any of the hypocrites of the world, but send instead one full of compassion and love, perhaps from a most unexpected source. Send to me one who will do for me what I cannot do for myself: let that person bandage my wounds, and cleanse them of ills, and place me upon the support of his own property, and bring me to a place of rest. Send me salvation and healing, O LORD, that I may glorify You.

In Thy Son's Name I pray, AMEN.

James 5:14-16

Is anyone among you sick? Then he must call for the elders of the church and they are to pray over him, anointing him with oil in the name of the Lord; and the prayer offered in faith will restore the one who is sick, and the Lord will raise him up, and if he has committed sins, they will be forgiven him. Therefore, confess your sins to one another, and pray for one another so that you may be healed. The effective prayer of a righteous man can accomplish much.

Dear Lord,

I offer my prayer in faith, O LORD, that my body may be healed of its ailments. I pray, too, for others who lie in sickness and pain, that they may likewise be healed. May our earnest prayers be heard in Your presence, O God, healing one another and saving us from our sins. Help me to confess my sins to You and to my fellow Christians that I may be forgiven; help me to pray for my fellows and they for me, that we may be healed in unity. Help me, too, to be righteous in Your sight through the sacrifice of Your Son, that my prayers may be answered to the fulfillment of Your will and the increase of Your glory.

In Thy Son's Name I pray, AMEN.

HEALING AND PEACE

Job 2:9-10

Then his wife said to him, "Do you still hold fast your integrity? Curse God and die!" But he said to her, "You speak as one of the foolish women speaks. Shall we indeed accept good from God and not accept adversity?" In all this Job did not sin with his lips.

Dear Lord,

Suffering and illness are a great struggle. I seek healing from my sores and pains, O LORD, but I seek foremost to remain faithful and to hold fast to my integrity. I often feel pressure, from those around me and from my own sinful self, to curse You that this suffering may alleviate in death; let me not fall into this evil, O God. Instead, let me accept adversity as well as good, hardship as well as ease. Do not let me sin with my lips, but let me be faithful to You always, that You may be glorified. Grant me wisdom, peace, and righteousness first; then, if it be Your will, grant me healing.

In Thy Son's Name I pray, AMEN.

Nahum 1:7

The LORD is good,
A stronghold in the day of trouble,
And He knows those who take refuge in Him.

Dear Lord,

I find myself lost and unprotected on this, my day of trouble. I am ill and I have no hope apart from You. Help me to find You, my stronghold. Rescue me from the sorrow and pain which beleaguers me. I seek to take refuge in You, O LORD. If, by Your will, that means that it is time for me to come home to You, then I pray for peace for myself and my family to accept this burden. But if it is not yet that time, if You still have tasks for me in this world, then I pray that You heal me and cure me of my sickness and disease. Not my will, but Thine be done, O LORD.

In Thy Son's Name I pray, AMEN.

John 16:33

"These things I have spoken to you, so that in Me you may have peace. In the world you have tribulation, but take courage; I have overcome the world."

Dear Lord,

This illness produces in me great worry. I fear for my life, and for the well-being of those who love me. Remind me of what You have done for me, as You explained it to Your disciples, so that I may have peace. I pray that You take away my diseases and cleanse my flesh, but whatever Your will is for my life, O God, I desire Your eternal peace, that both I and my loved ones can accept Your will in our lives. Help me to live my life, whether short or long—though I pray earnestly that it be long—according to that will, for Your glory and for my sanctification. Whether the future holds healing or not, it will be a time of tribulation; guide me in courage toward Your peace.

In Thy Son's Name I pray, AMEN.

HEALING AND SPIRITUAL GROWTH

John 9:2-3

And His disciples asked Him, "Rabbi, who sinned, this man or his parents, that he would be born blind?" Jesus answered, "It was neither that this man sinned, nor his parents; but it was so that the works of God might be displayed in him."

Dear Lord,

I seek Your peace. Help me to realize that sin is not the only cause for illness, but that it may be part of Your will, in order to mature us, to strengthen us, to make us holy, trusting in You first and ourselves after You. Shine Your light upon me, O God; work Your mighty works within me. Help me to be obedient to Your will, that I may be healed in body and soul, and moreover, that You may be glorified. Help me, like the man born blind, to see Your truth now, and give glory to You, praising You and thanking You always for healing me.

In Thy Son's Name I pray, AMEN.

1 Peter 4:12-13

Beloved, do not be surprised at the fiery ordeal among you, which comes upon you for your testing, as though some strange thing were happening to you; but to the degree that you share the sufferings of Christ, keep on rejoicing, so that also at the revelation of His glory you may rejoice with exultation.

Dear Lord,

This burning illness in me has brought struggle and tribulation upon me. Help me to see this hardship as the test that it is, instead of confusing it for some strange occurrence. Help me to realize that this test of faith is not some warranted punishment or arbitrary struggle. Guide me instead to persevere in faith, peace, humility, and love. As I share now in the pains and suffering of Christ on the cross, help me not to despair, but to rejoice in my participation with Christ. In this way, sanctify me for Your glory, that I may exult in the revelation of that glory. Heal me, O LORD, in Your timing; help me to mature and to grow as You have designed for me, that this test may serve its purpose in Your plan both for me and for those that love me. In this way, let me complete in my flesh what is wanting from the afflictions of Christ for the sake of His body, the Church. Let this be so that You may make known the abundance of the glory of Your word through my struggle according to Your will. Guide and direct me, O God, to fulfill Your will for my life, and heal me to Your glory.

In Thy Son's Name I pray, AMEN.

OTHER BOOKS WRITTEN BY NATHANIEL TURNER

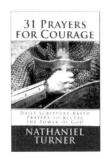

31 Prayers for Courage
Pray through struggles and fears in your life with these 31 prayers for courage. Find strength in God's Word.

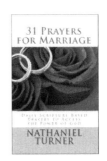

31 Prayers for Marriage
Pray with your spouse to strengthen the unity and love in your marriage with these 31 prayers for marriage. Find devotion and harmony through God's Word.

If you enjoyed this book, please review it on Amazon.com or send your comments to me (or both).

All of these books are available as eBooks on the Amazon Kindle!

Made in the USA
Middletown, DE
31 May 2015